W9-CMH-116

Allegheny Regional Asset
District Funds

THE SPANISH-AMERICAN WAR

12108

South Fayette Township Library
515 Millers Run Road
Morgan, PA 15064

In the most famous battle of the Spanish-American War,
Colonel Theodore Roosevelt leads the charge of the Rough
Riders near San Juan Hill on July 1, 1898. The picture is by
the well-known artist Frederic Remington (1861–1909).

IMPERIAL AMBITIONS

THE

SPANISH-AMERICAN

WAR

ALDEN R. CARTER

FRANKLIN WATTS

New York ★ Chicago ★ London ★ Toronto ★ Sydney

A First Book

ACKNOWLEDGMENTS

Many thanks to all who helped with *The Spanish-American War,* particularly my editor, Reni Roxas; my mother, Hilda Carter Fletcher; and my friends Barbara Feinberg and Dean Markwardt. As always, my wife, Carol, deserves much of the credit.

Maps by William J. Clipson

Cover photograph copyright © The Bettmann Archive

Photographs copyright © : New York Public Library, Picture Collection: pp. 2, 8, 14, 16, 22, 28, 39, 40, 42, 45, 49; Brown Brothers, Sterling, PA: pp. 8 (inset), 27, 34, 37; The Bettmann Archive: pp. 13, 19, 25, 33, 36, 47, 51, 54, 58; UPI/Bettmann Newsphotos: p. 56.

Library of Congress Cataloging-in-Publication Data

Carter, Alden R.
The Spanish-American War / by Alden R. Carter.
p.   cm. — (A First book)
Includes bibliographical references and index.
Summary: Chronicles the sixteen-week war in 1898 between the United States and Spain over the liberation of Cuba, the outcome of which ended the Spanish colonial empire and elevated the United States to a world power.
ISBN 0-531-20078-7 (lib. bdg.) / ISBN 0-531-15657-5 (pbk.)
1. Spanish-American War, 1898—Juvenile literature. [1. Spanish-American War, 1898.] I.Title. II. Series.
E715.C37   1992
973.8'9—dc20   91-14753 CIP AC

Copyright © 1992 by Alden R. Carter
All rights reserved
Printed in the United States of America
6   5   4   3

CONTENTS

FOR
JUDY, MARK,
AND DAVID

ONE

REMEMBER THE *MAINE*

ON THE warm evening of February 15, 1898, a great white ship lay at anchor in the harbor of Havana, Cuba. The lights of the city and the stars in the clear sky reflected on the gentle waters lapping the sides of the battleship USS *Maine*. Aboard, all was peaceful. Most of the crew had already rolled into their hammocks, leaving only the watch and a few idlers above decks to enjoy the calm tropical night.

Things were not so peaceful outside the capital of Spain's troubled colony. In the countryside, a rebel army under General Máximo Gómez fought to win Cuba's independence. At sixty-two, the thin, white-haired Gómez looked frail, but he was tough in body and spirit. His small army moved fast, hitting lonely Spanish forts and patrols, burning sugarcane fields and mills, then fading into the hills and jungles.

The Spanish army hunted the rebels, fighting to save this small piece of Spain's once mighty empire. A century before, Spain had ruled Central America, all of South America except Brazil, many of the Caribbean islands, Mexico, and all of North America west of the Mississippi River. But European wars in the first part of the nineteenth century drained Spain's power. Nearly all of Spain's colonies declared their independence. The United States took by purchase or force the vast lands Spain had once claimed in North America. But Spain refused American offers to buy Cuba, the rich island 90 miles (145 km) south of Florida. Through decades of war and unrest at home and abroad, Spain clung stubbornly to Cuba and Puerto Rico—all that remained of its empire in the New World.

American adventurers—called "filibusters," from a Spanish term for sea raiders—tried to stir the Cuban people to revolt. The United States ignored Spanish protests when filibustering increased after the American Civil War (1861–65). In 1868 the eastern half of Cuba rose in a revolt called the

Cuban rebels salute the flag
of a free Cuba before battle in this
drawing by Frederic Remington.
The officer on the white horse
is probably General Máximo Gómez.
Inset: Hard and tough as old leather,
General Máximo Gómez (1836–1905)
led the rebels in their fight to free
Cuba from the Spaniards.

Ten Years' War (1868–78). Filibuster ships, often flying the American flag, brought money, guns, and recruits to the rebels. In 1873 the Spaniards captured the filibuster ship *Virginius*. Over the objections of the United States, Spanish authorities in the port of Santiago de Cuba tried and shot fifty-two of the crew.

President Ulysses S. Grant ordered the United States Navy to gather at Key West, Florida, for a showdown with Spain. Long short of funds, the American navy could muster only an embarrassing collection of leaky hulks. Both nations backed away from war. Five years later, the Cuban rebels gave up the fight.

Máximo Gómez and a few other revolutionaries refused to accept defeat. After years of planning and raising support in the United States, they declared a new revolution early in 1895. Faced with the worst threat yet to Spanish rule, Cuba's governor, General Valeriano Weyler, began a brutal "reconcentration" program to empty the countryside of the poor farmers who provided the rebel army with food, clothing, and recruits. Spanish soldiers herded more than a million people into bare, dirty camps where some 400,000 died of hunger and disease.

Reports of the misery in Cuba brought an outcry in the United States. Newspapers urged President William McKinley—a gentle, peace-loving man—to take military action to rescue the Cuban people. Fearing war with the powerful United States, the Spanish government recalled Weyler and sent a peace offer to the rebels. But Weyler's removal was unpopular with army officers and wealthy Cubans; rioters stormed through the streets of Havana, accusing the government of caving in to the demands of the rebels and the North Americans. The rioting threatened American citizens and business interests in Cuba. To show the power of the United States, McKinley ordered the *Maine* to Havana in late January 1898.

The president had another reason for sending the battleship. German warships were cruising the waters of the Caribbean, and Germany made no secret of its desire for colonies to match those of Great Britain and France. The presence of the *Maine* would warn the Germans that the United States was not going to let them grab Cuba without a fight.

To McKinley's relief, Havana greeted the arrival of the *Maine* calmly. The *Maine* was one of six modern battleships in the small but growing United States Navy. One of the strongest backers of a large navy was a human volcano of physical and mental energy named Theodore Roosevelt. Unlike McKinley, Roosevelt, the thirty-eight-year-old assistant secretary of the navy, longed for war with Spain.

Roosevelt believed in expanding America's power and territory—a political theory called *expansionism*. Since the Civil War, the United States had grown into one of the wealthiest nations on earth. Millions of immigrants poured in from Europe. Railroads and settlements spread across the North American continent to the Pacific Ocean. New cities blossomed almost overnight. As the nineteenth century drew to a close, a dizzying assortment of recent inventions—the telephone, the electric light, the phonograph, the first automobile, the wireless telegraph, and a hundred others—revolutionized daily life. America was feeling its oats. Bursting with talent, energy, and ambition, the United States seemed chosen to lead the world into a new age.

For Roosevelt and his fellow "expansionists," America's future lay in building an overseas empire. Colonies would provide markets for America's booming factories, while American rule would lift the "backward" peoples of distant lands out of poverty and ignorance. To win and protect an empire, the United States would need a large fleet, overseas bases, and a canal across Central America to move ships between the Atlantic and Pacific oceans. Cuba sat in the middle of the shipping lanes that would feed the canal—and that made the island far too important to leave in Spanish hands.

While the *Maine's* officers attended parties and bullfights in Havana, Roosevelt prepared the navy for war. He warned friends that he would leave his desk job at the first shot. No one who knew Roosevelt doubted him; "T.R." loved a challenge. A sickly child, he had built himself into a rugged outdoorsman, written numerous history books, held a seat in the New York legislature, ranched in Dakota Territory, and served on the U.S. Civil Service Board and as police

Expansionists imagined Cuba as a future territory
of the United States. In this 1897 cartoon,
Uncle Sam says: "I ain't in a hurry, it'll drop
into my basket when it gets ripe."

On the evening of February 15, 1898,
a powerful explosion ripped through the battleship
USS *Maine* as it lay at anchor in Havana harbor.

commissioner of New York City. Somehow he found time to be a devoted husband and father of five. His flashing eyes behind wire-rimmed glasses and his big grin beneath a walrus mustache showed his love of life. Teddy Roosevelt planned to write his name large in the history of his country.

Roosevelt was not alone in urging the United States to throw Spain out of the Western Hemisphere. The colorful newspaper owners William Randolph Hearst and Joseph Pulitzer thought a small war would be good for newspaper sales. Their rival papers competed fiercely in printing sensational — and often invented — stories about the fighting and suffering in Cuba.

On the night of February 15, 1898, as the *Maine* lay quietly at anchor in Havana, Hearst attended a party in New York City, unaware that he would soon have the biggest story of his career to report. The *Maine's* bugler blew taps. In his cabin, Captain Charles D. Sigsbee paused to listen before continuing a letter to his wife. At 9:40 P.M., a roar shook the ship. An instant later, a second explosion shot a tower of flame skyward. The great ship lifted clear of the water, then — its back broken — plunged toward the bottom of Havana harbor.

Newspaper publisher William Randolph Hearst (1863–1951)
told the artist Frederic Remington: "You furnish
the pictures and I'll furnish the war."

TWO

"THIS MEANS WAR!"

RETURNING home from the party late that night, William Randolph Hearst heard the news of the sinking of the *Maine*. "This means war!" he snapped. The next morning, his *New York Journal* splashed the story across its entire front page. A day later, the *Journal's* headline screamed, "The Warship Maine Was Split in Two by an Enemy's Secret Infernal Machine"; on the following day, "The Whole Country Thrills with the War Fever."

While American newspapers howled, the *Maine* rested in the mud of Havana harbor, only its masts and twisted superstructure above water. The explosion had killed 262 crewmen. Spanish sailors had risked their lives to pull one hundred survivors from the water. Clara Barton, founder of the American Red Cross, visited the hospitals and reported that Spanish doctors were doing their utmost to save the wounded.

Spanish investigators guessed that a fire in one of the *Maine's* coal-storage bunkers had touched off explosives in a nearby ammunition magazine. Every sailor knew that coal stored for long periods could begin smoldering by a process called spontaneous combustion. However, Captain Sigsbee insisted that the *Maine's* coal had been fresh and that the outside steel walls of the bunker had been cool to the touch. Sigsbee told investigators that he thought an underwater mine had blown the gaping hole in the bottom of his ship.

Teddy Roosevelt was too impatient to wait for investigators' reports. He began buying and arming merchant ships to carry an army to Cuba. To strengthen the navy's Caribbean squadron, he ordered the USS *Oregon*—the navy's mightiest battleship—to make ready for the 16,000-mile (26,000-km) voyage from San Francisco, around South America, to Cuban waters. Looking even farther afield, he sent a cable to Commodore George Dewey ordering the navy's Far Eastern squadron to prepare for an attack on the Spanish fleet in the Philippine Islands.

Investigators crawled over the wreckage of the *Maine*. The Spaniards blamed an accidental fire for the explosion. The Americans suspected an underwater mine. In all likelihood, the Spaniards were correct.

Few Americans knew much about this Spanish colony on the far side of the Pacific Ocean. Tensions had been rising between the Filipinos and their colonial masters for many years. In 1896 the government tried and shot the peaceful reformer and writer Dr. José Rizal on a trumped-up charge of treason. Outraged Filipinos took up arms against the Spaniards. General Emilio Aguinaldo led daring raids against Spanish outposts until, short of men and supplies, he was forced to flee the Philippines early in 1898.

Roosevelt had little interest in the success of the Philippine revolution; he was imagining the islands as an American colony. Only 700 miles (1,100 km) from the British colony of Hong Kong, the capital city of Manila would make an ideal base for the American navy, while the Philippines became both a rich market for American goods and a bridge to China, the world's biggest market. In Roosevelt's expansionist dreams, the Philippines would be America's stepping stone to world power.

In Washington, D.C., Congress debated the question of war with Spain. On March 17, Senator Redfield Proctor of Vermont delivered a quiet, no-nonsense report on his recent visit to Cuba. Coming from the moderate Proctor, the description of the terrible suffering in Cuba horrified the Senate. That same day the American investigators of the *Maine* sinking sent their conclusions to President McKinley. After careful study, they agreed with Captain Sigsbee: an underwater mine had caused the explosion. Who had placed it they did not know.

Seventy-eight years later, American naval engineers would disprove the mine theory and side with the Spanish explanation of the explosion; but in the spring of 1898, most Americans blamed a Spanish plot. With the press and the public screaming for revenge, McKinley sent a list of demands to the Spanish government. Spain had every reason to avoid war and agreed to every condition for peace except the last one — independence for Cuba. After four hundred years of empire in the Americas, Spain could not swallow this final blow to its pride.

Spain asked the European powers for help, but mighty Great Britain sided with the United States and the other European nations excused themselves. Spain would have to face the United States on its own. On April 11, 1898, McKinley asked Congress for the authority to use force in Cuba. Eight days later Congress agreed, stating clearly that the goal of the United States was independence for Cuba, not the gaining of a colony. On April 22, American warships began blockading Havana. Facing almost hopeless odds, Spain declared war.

The first battle of the Spanish-American war was fought on the other side of the world from Cuba. Following Roosevelt's instructions, Commodore Dewey sailed for the Philippines on April 29 with a squadron of four armored cruisers,

Two months after the sinking of the *Maine*,
President William McKinley (1843–1901)
signed an ultimatum demanding that Spain
withdraw its army from Cuba and grant
independence to the Cuban people.

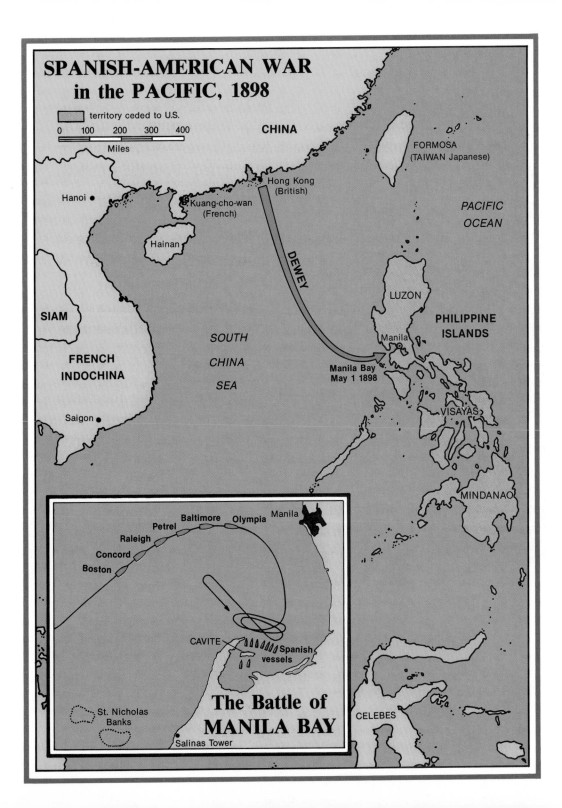

SPANISH-AMERICAN WAR in the PACIFIC, 1898

territory ceded to U.S.

0   100   200   300   400
Miles

CHINA

FORMOSA
(TAIWAN Japanese)

Hanoi

Kuang-cho-wan
(French)

Hong Kong
(British)

PACIFIC
OCEAN

Hainan

DEWEY

LUZON

SIAM

SOUTH

FRENCH
INDOCHINA

CHINA

Manila

PHILIPPINE
ISLANDS

SEA

Manila Bay
May 1 1898

Saigon

VISAYAS

MINDANAO

The Battle of MANILA BAY

Manila

Baltimore   Olympia
Petrel
Raleigh
Concord
Boston

CAVITE

Spanish
vessels

St. Nicholas
Banks

CELEBES

Salinas Tower

three smaller warships, and two unarmed coal tenders. Although the cruisers were outdated ships equipped with both steam engines and tall masts for sails, they were manned by first-rate crews. Some officers worried about the rumored size of the Spanish fleet, but the short, dapper Dewey had no doubts of victory.

In the early morning hours of May 1, Dewey's ships slipped past the guns of the Spanish shore batteries along a narrow channel into Manila Bay. A flare of burning soot from a stack on one of the ships alerted the Spanish gunners. The shore batteries roared, but an answering storm of shells from the Americans smashed the Spanish guns.

The Spanish admiral, Patricio Montojo y Pasarón, watched Dewey's battle line steaming through the dawn toward his anchored squadron. Montojo was badly outgunned. He had only two large cruisers (one of them wooden), four smaller cruisers, and three gunboats. He kept his ships at anchor near the shore, gloomily hoping that Dewey would make a fatal error. At 5:40 A.M., with the range to the Spanish ships down to 2.5 miles (4 km), Dewey turned to the captain of his flagship *Olympia:* "You may fire when you are ready, Gridley."

From the flying bridge of his flagship *Olympia,* Commodore George Dewey (1837–1917) directs American fire in the battle of Manila Bay on May 1, 1898.

The crash of the *Olympia*'s big guns shook the decks and shattered the peace of the morning. The American ships steamed back and forth, pounding their easy targets. Montojo's ships burst into flames, but the Spanish sailors stuck stubbornly to their guns. One of Dewey's officers recalled: "The red-and-yellow flag of Spain still flew above the shattered, burning hulks, and their broadsides flashed defiantly."

Montojo's flagship, the *Reina Cristina,* cut its anchor chain and hobbled out to take on the *Olympia.* At the range of one-half mile (four-fifths km), the *Olympia* reduced the *Cristina* to a smoking wreck. After two hours, the American ships turned away to resupply their ammunition. The American crews ate breakfast as Spain's brave sailors dragged their dead and wounded from their blasted ships. Shortly after 11:00 A.M., the Americans resumed firing. Under the rain of shells, the Spaniards raised a white flag.

At a cost of only eight wounded, Dewey had destroyed the Spanish fleet, killed or wounded nearly four hundred Spanish sailors, and broken Spanish power in the Philippines. Manila lay before him for the taking, but he had no troops to send ashore.

In the strange twilight of Spain's Far Eastern empire, the Spaniards held Manila for another three months, praying for rescue from their distant homeland. Dewey's ships lay at anchor, waiting for the arrival of an American army from California. German warships steamed into the harbor,

Badly outgunned by Dewey's squadron,
Admiral Patricio Montojo tried to fight with
his ships anchored close to shore. The
Americans pounded the Spanish ships into
smoking wrecks in less than three hours.

1,011,068
Per Week-Day April Average.
GAIN in One Year - - 338,748
"Circulation Books Open to All."

The World.

1,011,068
Per Week-Day April Average.
GAIN in Three Years - 461,205

The World's Greatest Christmas Record!

"Circulation Books Open to All."

VOL. XXXVIII. NO. 13,404.

[Copyright, 1898, by the Press Publishing Company, New York World.]

NEW YORK, MONDAY, MAY 2, 1898.

PRICE

DEWEY SMASHES SPAIN'S FLEET

VICE-ADMIRAL MONTOJO.

The Defeated Commander of the Spanish Fleet.

Great Naval Battle Between Asiatic Squadron and Spanish Warships Off Manila.

THREE OF THE BEST SPANISH VESSELS WIPED OUT, OTHERS SUNK.

The Damage Done to the American Boats Engaged Only Nominal---Hundreds of the Enemy Slain in the Encounter.

COMMODORE DEWEY.

Winner of First Great Victory for New American Navy.

LISBON, Portugal, May 1, 11 P. M.----The Spanish fleet was completely defeated off Cavite, Philippine Islands, according to trustworthy advices received here.

WASHINGTON, May 1, Midnight.---President McKinley expresses entire satisfaction over the reported battle between Commodore Dewey's squadron and the Spanish fleet He accepts the news as true, but believes it is worse for the Spanish than they will admit. There has been no official confirmation of the news. Nothing official is expected for forty-eight hours.

THE THREE SPANISH CRUISERS COMPLETELY DESTROYED.

CASTILLA.

DON JUAN DE AUSTRIA.

SPANISH FLAG-SHIP
"REINA MARIA CRISTINA."

FLYING SQUADRON STRENGTHENED.

(Special to The World.)

FORT MONROE, May 1.—The converted yacht Scorpion, in charge of Lieut.-Commander Marix, joined the Flying Squadron in Hampton Roads at 1 P. M. to-day after a quick trip from New York. The Scorpion's arrival greatly pleased Commodore Schley, as the Squadron, while strong in heavy fighting ships, is weak in swift, lightsarmed craft.

Chaplain Jones, the "fighting parson" of the Texas, preached a red-hot war sermon to-day to the officers and men of the battleship. He took his text from the thirty-second chapter of Deuteronomy, starting from the eighteenth to the forty-third verse, inclusive.

"Ye shall see if these verses had been written in order as an admonition to Spain, their appropriateness could not have been more emphatic, especially—

He said I will hide my face from them; I will see what their end shall be; for they are a very froward generation, children in whom is no faith.

"They shall be burnt with hunger and shall with burning heat and with bitter destruction.

"The time hath a month of cursing and they are wise; that they understand their latter end!

"O that they were wise, that they understood this, that they would consider their latter end!

"Nothing at known as to when the floating battery is to do its work.

The work of laying mines and torpedoes in the harbor continued all day.

Pennsylvania Railroad Excursion

Improved and complete bar fare and a complete bar... Every Wednesday... until the advent.

ADMIRAL MONTOJO ADMITS HIS UTTER ROUT.

In His Report to Spain He Says Many Ships Were Burned and Sunk and the Losses in Officers and Men "Numerous."

MADRID (via Paris), May 2.—The time of the retreat of the American squadron behind the merchantmen was 11.30 A. M. The American squadron forced the port before daybreak and appeared off Cavite. Night was completely dark.

The Naval Bureau at Manila sends the following report, signed "Montojo, Admiral:"

"In the middle of the night the American squadron forced the forts, and before daybreak appeared off Cavite. The night was completely dark. At 7.30 the bow of the Reina Christina took fire, and soon after the poop also was burned.

"At eight o'clock, with my staff, I went on board the Isla de Cuba. The Reina Maria Christina and the Castilla were then entirely enveloped in flames.

"The other ships having been damaged retired into Baker Bay. Some had to be sunk to prevent their falling into the hands of the enemy. The losses are numerous, notably Capt. Cadarso, a priest, and nine other persons.

"The Spaniards fought splendidly, the sailors refusing to leave the burning and sinking Don Juan de Austria. There is the greatest anxiety for further details.

MADRID'S FORLORN HOPE.

LONDON, May 2.—The Madrid correspondent of the Financial News, telegraphing this morning, says:

"The Spanish Ministry of Marine claims a victory for Spain because the Americans were forced to retire behind the merchantmen. Capt. Cadalso (or Cadarso), in command of the Reina Maria Christina, went down with the ship.

MADRID OFFICIAL REPORT ADMITS DISASTROUS DEFEAT

(Despatch Sanctioned by Spanish Government and Passed by the Censor.)

MADRID, May 1, 8 P. M.---The following is the text of the official despatch from the Governor-General of the Philippine Islands to the Minister of War, Lieut.-Gen. Correa, regarding the engagement off Manila:

"Last night, April 30, the batteries at the entrance to the fort announced the arrival of the enemy's squadron, forcing a passage under the obscurity of the night.

"At daybreak the enemy took up positions, opening with a strong fire against Fort Cavite and the arsenal.

"Our fleet engaged the enemy in a brilliant combat, protecte

(Continued on Second Page.)

landing officers to hold mysterious talks with the Spanish authorities. Dewey could only wonder if one day a whistle of shells would announce that Germany had gone to war on the side of Spain. General Aguinaldo returned to the Philippines, believing that he had a promise of American support. His rebels surrounded Manila, and Aguinaldo declared the Philippines a republic on June 12. He invited Dewey to the ceremony, but the American commodore declined. Aguinaldo could only suspect that Philippine independence did not quite fit with America's dream of world power.

Joseph Pulitzer's New York newspaper *The World* celebrated the American triumph in the battle of Manila Bay. Commodore Dewey became an admiral and a national hero.

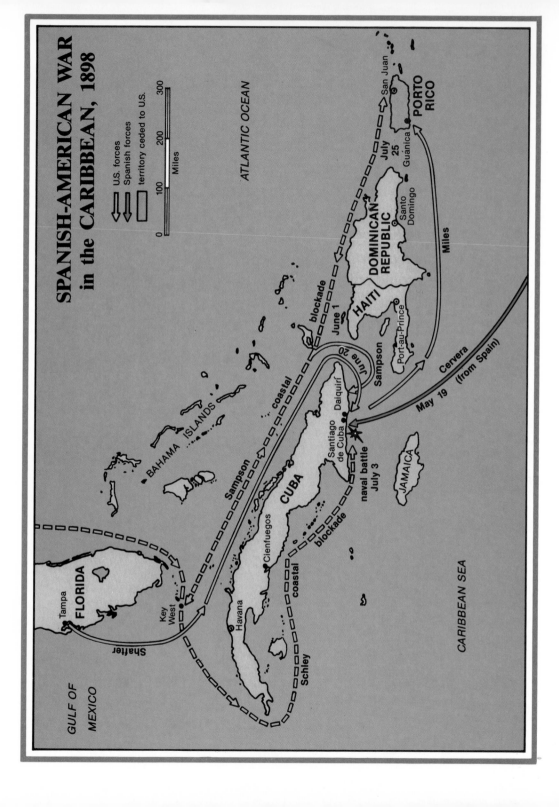

THREE

THE FIGHT FOR CUBA

TRUE to his word, Teddy Roosevelt left his desk job for the war early in May 1898. He rode the train to San Antonio, Texas, to join the First Volunteer Cavalry as second-in-command to his friend Dr. Leonard Wood. Like other officers, Colonel Wood and Lieutenant Colonel Roosevelt faced the job of turning civilians into soldiers in a few short weeks.

With a peacetime strength of only twenty-eight thousand soldiers, the army was ill-prepared for the quarter-million recruits who answered the president's call for volunteers. They were given hot woolen uniforms, served inedible "embalmed beef," and issued old-fashioned rifles with black-powder shells that spouted easy-to-spot clouds of smoke. For army pay of thirteen dollars a month, the eager recruits would risk hardship, Spanish bullets, and—most dangerous of all—disease.

True to his word, Teddy Roosevelt (1858–1919)
quit his desk job as assistant secretary of the
navy to join the army for the fight in Cuba.
This studio photograph shows Roosevelt in the
uniform of a lieutenant colonel of volunteers.

In the jungles of Cuba, people unused to the tropical climate caught any of a dozen severe illnesses. Most feared was yellow fever, a deadly sickness that could sweep through an army in days. In 1898 no one knew that "yellow jack" was spread by mosquitoes, but everyone knew that the risk of a major outbreak increased during the summer rainy season. The army wanted to wait until the fall before landing troops in Cuba. The navy argued for a spring invasion to avoid the autumn hurricane season. President McKinley sided with the navy.

The news cheered the impatient recruits of the First Volunteer Cavalry. Nicknamed the Rough Riders, they were a tough bunch from the Southwest—with a sprinkling of Easterners like Roosevelt—who much preferred fighting to drilling. At the end of May they boarded the train for Tampa, Florida, where the rest of the army was gathering for an expedition to capture Havana. But the invasion plans hit a snag. A Spanish naval squadron under Admiral Pascual Cervera y Topete was loose in the Caribbean. The navy told the army to wait until it found and destroyed Cervera's ships.

Cervera was an unwilling warrior. His handful of rundown ships hardly matched the rumors of an awesome fleet about to swoop down on the coast of the United States. Before leaving Spain, the tiny, aging admiral had warned his government that a battle with the American navy could only lead to the pointless death of his sailors. The government disregarded his warnings and ordered the squadron to sea. Heartsick, Cervera obeyed.

Low on coal and badly needing repairs, the Spanish ships limped into the Caribbean in the second week of May. After ducking into the remote islands of Martinique and Curaçao, the squadron slipped through the American blockade to drop anchor in the safe harbor of Santiago de Cuba on the southeast coast of Cuba.

Unwilling to sacrifice his weak squadron in a
pointless battle, Admiral Pascual Cervera (1839–1909)
eluded the American fleet and brought his ships
safely to the protected waters of Santiago de Cuba.

On May 28, Rear Admiral William T. Sampson's powerful American squadron found Cervera's hiding place. But the American battleships could not get at the four Spanish cruisers. El Morro fort guarded the narrow channel into Santiago harbor, its guns ready to blast any ship trying to pass without permission. The wily Cervera had put Sampson in a fix. The American army needed Sampson's ships to protect a landing on the northwest coast near Havana, yet he could not leave the Spanish cruisers free to raid at will.

Sampson asked a young naval officer, Richmond Hobson, to carry out a bold plan to block the harbor mouth. Under the cover of dark, Hobson would take the coal transport *Merrimac* past El Morro, swing the ship broadside in the channel, and sink it with a series of explosive charges. Like a stopper in a bottle, the sunken *Merrimac* would trap the Spanish ships inside the harbor.

Early on the morning of June 3, Hobson and a crew of seven volunteers steered to within a mile (1.6 km) of Morro Point. Moonlight silvered the water, making the unarmed *Merrimac* a perfect target. Hobson ordered full-speed ahead, and the ship surged forward. Spanish sentries shouted an alarm, and cannons roared from the shore. A Spanish patrol boat gave chase, firing at the *Merrimac's* rudder. The walls of the channel loomed ahead. Hobson gave the command to stop engines, and the *Merrimac* coasted into the narrow opening. "Hard aport," Hobson yelled. Nothing happened; the Spanish shells had shot away the steering gear. The desperate Hobson ordered the charges fired, but only two of the ten went off.

Settling slowly, the *Merrimac* slid clear of the narrows and into the harbor. Hobson and his men threw themselves flat on the deck as Spanish shells rained about them. Two torpedoes blew huge holes in the sides of the wounded ship. The bow plunged, and a rush of water swept the eight Americans over the side. Amazingly, Hobson and his men survived unhurt. At dawn a passing boat hauled them from the water. A short, white-bearded officer congratulated them for a "valiant" attempt—a brave man himself, Admiral Cervera knew valiant men when he met them.

Lieutenant Richmond Hobson tried to bottle up Cervera's ships in port by sinking the collier *Merrimac* in the harbor entrance. Although the attempt failed, its bravery made heroes of Hobson and his men.

Sampson next tried to knock out El Morro with his ships' heavy guns, but the shells did little damage to the fort's stout walls. It would take the American army to capture Santiago and force Cervera's ships to surrender or fight.

On June 7, the U.S. army began loading onto ships in Tampa Bay, Florida. The port was an incredible tangle of men and supplies. Stranded far up the single railroad line, the Rough Riders risked missing the fight in Cuba. But Teddy Roosevelt stepped onto the tracks and forced a north-bound coal train to stop. He ordered the Rough Riders aboard and instructed the engineer in friendly but firm tones to back the train the 9 miles (14.5 km) to the port. Roosevelt chose the first empty ship and sent the Rough Riders up the gang-plank. When the soldiers assigned to the ship arrived, the Rough Riders refused to get off.

Unable to destroy Cervera's Spanish squadron in Santiago harbor, Rear Admiral William T. Sampson (1840–1902) had to call on the army to take the city by land.

Jammed into the transports, the army waited a week in blazing Florida heat while the navy checked out the false sighting of another Spanish squadron. Finally, the army sailed for Cuba. Left behind were most of the Rough Riders' horses; except for Roosevelt and Wood, the First Volunteer Cavalry would fight on foot.

The thirty-two transports arrived off Santiago on the morning of June 21. Major General W. Rufus Shafter commanded the sixteen thousand soldiers aboard. At sixty-three, Shafter seemed an odd choice to lead the army. Of only average height, he weighed over 300 pounds (136 kg), could not mount a horse without help, and suffered terribly in the tropical heat.

Shafter and Sampson went ashore to meet General Calixto García, the rebel commander in the area. The three officers decided to land the army at the small port of Daiquirí, 18 miles (29 km) east of Santiago. On the morning of June 22, Sampson's warships pounded Daiquirí's old fort until a rebel patrol signaled from the beach that the Spaniards had already abandoned the town.

The portly Major General W. Rufus Shafter (1835–1906) and the slender Admiral Sampson are greeted by cheering Cuban rebels as they arrive to plan the American landing with General Calixto García.

The unloading began. Long lines of boats carried the troops ashore. Horses were pushed over the sides of the ships to swim to land. Naked soldiers in the surf wrestled supplies onto the sand. The landing cost the lives of two men and a number of horses drowned, but by midnight half the army stood on Cuban soil. The next morning, an American regiment captured the town of Siboney, 7 miles (11.3 km) closer to Santiago, to give the army a second and better port.

With every day bringing the season of rain and yellow fever closer, Shafter wasted no time moving on Santiago.

The American army landed unopposed at the small port of Daiquirí on June 22, 1898.

On the morning of June 24, the Rough Riders got their first taste of war. Cutting their way through thick jungle toward the crossroads of Las Guásimas, they came under heavy fire from well-hidden Spanish soldiers. Crawling forward foot by foot, the Rough Riders and two other regiments forced the Spaniards to retreat.

The Spaniards withdrew to the Santiago defenses. The Americans followed, dragging their cannons and supplies along narrow jungle roads through choking dust, thick mud, and swarms of biting insects. Finally, the army's scouts broke into open ground and stared up at the San Juan Heights guarding Santiago. From trenches and concrete blockhouses, the Spanish soldiers stared back.

On June 30, Shafter studied the Spanish positions from the village of El Pozo, 1.5 miles (2.4 km) from the San Juan Heights. General Arsenio Linares had 10,500 Spanish soldiers to defend Santiago, but his lines were long and the Americans could strike where they chose. Shafter called his generals together and told them his plan: At dawn the next day, an infantry division under General Henry W. Lawton would attack the Spanish stronghold at the village of El Caney, 6 miles (9.7 km) north of Santiago. General García's Cubans would cut the road to Santiago to keep Linares from sending more troops to El Caney. Once El Caney was taken—a task Lawton estimated would take no more than two hours—the entire army would charge the San Juan Heights.

Black cavalrymen led by white officers fought
gallantly at Las Guásimas and later in the attack
on the San Juan Heights. Like the Rough Riders,
they had left their horses in Florida.

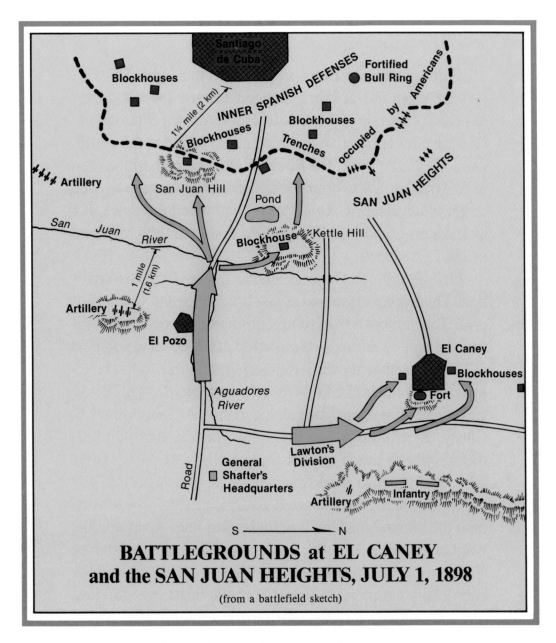

**BATTLEGROUNDS at EL CANEY
and the SAN JUAN HEIGHTS, JULY 1, 1898**

(from a battlefield sketch)

In their attack on Santiago, the Americans stormed
El Caney and the San Juan Heights on July 1, 1898.
The Rough Riders' charge that day was up Kettle Hill.
The American lines are seen, at top, after the heights were won.

Through the late afternoon and into the night, Shafter's sixteen thousand soldiers slogged toward the battlefield along the crowded jungle roads. Horse-drawn cannons and Gatling guns (primitive machine guns) added to the confusion. Well after dark, the Rough Riders turned off the road at El Pozo for a few hours' rest. Roosevelt was too excited to get much sleep. Colonel Wood had taken the place of a sick general, and Roosevelt would command the regiment in the fight ahead.

First light found General Shafter unable to rise from his bed. The tropical heat had at last broken the fat, aging general. Too stubborn to give up command, he decided to direct the battle with reports gathered at the observation post at El Pozo and sent over a field-telephone line to his headquarters 3.5 miles (5.6 km) from the battlefield. At 6:30 A.M. Lawton's 5,400 Americans attacked the 520 Spaniards at El Caney. In minutes the Americans learned that numbers meant only so much against stone walls, trenches, barbed wire, and Spanish marksmanship. The attack stalled.

To the south, ten thousand American soldiers crowded onto the narrow road leading to the San Juan River and the heights beyond. At 8:00 A.M. American cannons started shelling the heights. Spanish artillery replied with quick and deadly counterfire. Spanish shells burst over the jungle, and jagged fragments tore into the tightly packed American troops. An American officer stupidly ordered the army's observation balloon towed forward. The fat, yellow

This fanciful picture of the American attack on
El Caney gets many of the details wrong but captures
the savagery of the fight. Outnumbered ten to one,
the Spaniards fought to nearly the last man.

balloon floating over the trees gave the Spanish riflemen a
perfect marker to identify the position of the American
troops marching along the hidden road. The Spaniards
doubled their fire; dozens, then scores, of Americans fell
dead or wounded.

Up ahead, Roosevelt saw what was happening as the balloon made its slow, deadly way forward. He ordered the Rough Riders across the river and to the right end of the American line forming at the foot of the heights. Hiding in brush and tall grass, the soldiers waited for the order to charge. No order came. To the north, Lawton's men were making little headway at El Caney, and—far to the rear—General Shafter had lost control of his plan. More American regiments straggled into line, their ranks thinning by the minute under the Spanish fire.

Noon passed, and still the men waited. At 1:00 P.M. Lieutenant John D. Miley, a young officer on Shafter's staff, stood in a small crowd of generals and colonels. It was his job to pass on the order to attack, but no messenger could get to him over the bullet-swept road stretching back to El Pozo. Miley swallowed hard and gave the order to charge.

The Rough Riders and two regiments of black cavalry on foot charged up steep Kettle Hill in a ragged line. Roosevelt galloped ahead on his horse, Little Texas. He leaped from the saddle and scrambled over a wire fence 40 yards (37 m) from the top. The Rough Riders came on behind, feet slipping on the grass, hearts pounding, lungs gasping. Soldiers fell as Spanish bullets smacked into flesh, but there were too many Americans for the few Spaniards in the trenches ahead. The Spaniards ran as the Rough Riders swarmed over the top of the hill.

To the left, the line advancing up San Juan Hill slowed

The image of sabre-swinging Rough Riders charging
San Juan Hill on horseback became a popular myth.
Actually, the Rough Riders stormed nearby Kettle Hill
on foot and without awkward, outdated swords.

under heavy fire. Then a sudden drumming announced the arrival of the American Gatling guns. Thousands of bullets swept the Spanish trenches and blockhouse. The American line surged forward, rolling over the top of the hill. With a hoarse cheer, the Rough Riders joined the charge down into the valley and up the next line of hills. The Spaniards emptied their rifles at the Americans and fled.

The Stars and Stripes flew over the San Juan Heights an hour after Miley gave the order to charge. El Caney finally fell to the Americans two hours later. The day of bloody fighting cost 205 American dead and another 1,180 wounded, against Spanish losses of 215 dead and 376 wounded. In the gloomy aftermath, the battle seemed an empty victory. The Americans had cracked only the outer defenses of Santiago, not the far stronger inner ring.

Hungry and thirsty, tortured by insects and the blazing sun, the Americans scraped shallow trenches in the rocky hills overlooking the city. The Spaniards still had nearly ten thousand men in Santiago and could counterattack at any time, smashing through the thin American lines and scattering the army. Shafter considered pulling back to a safer distance, but his generals voted to hold on to the small gains won with so much blood.

General José Toral, who had taken over for the wounded Linares, was too discouraged to attack. Santiago was short of food and crowded with thousands of trapped civilians. Many of Toral's soldiers were too sick to fight. He wired his

The Rough Riders gathered around Colonel Theodore Roosevelt
for a photograph after the battle on July 1, 1898.
The cost of the fight seems to weigh on many minds;
Roosevelt looks distracted, and few of the men can
manage more than half-hearted smiles.

government that to defend the city was hopeless. Admiral Cervera had long believed that the whole war was hopeless, yet there remained the matter of Spanish pride. On the morning of July 3, Cervera's little squadron steamed out of Santiago to make the final blood sacrifice for Spain's honor.

The American warships lay in a wide semicircle outside the harbor. Admiral Sampson had taken the heavy cruiser *New York* west to Siboney for a meeting with Shafter. The crews of the other ships were enjoying a peaceful Sunday morning when a lookout on the heavy cruiser *Brooklyn* spotted smoke in the Santiago channel. An officer yelled to Commodore Winfield S. Schley, the senior officer in Sampson's absence: "The enemy's ships are coming out!" Alarms rang on the American ships, sending their crews racing for battle stations.

With black hulls gleaming and decks scoured bright, the four Spanish cruisers and two destroyers steamed into the open ocean flying the red-and-gold battle flag of Spain. Aboard Cervera's flagship, the *Infanta Maria Teresa,* Captain Victor Concas murmured, "Poor Spain!" Cervera made a sad, helpless gesture.

The American ships moved in for the kill. The *Maria Teresa* traded shots with the battleship *Iowa,* then swung west to race along the coast, the other Spanish ships falling in behind. Outgunned three to one, the Spaniards could only hope that speed would save them. The American ships pounded along on a parallel course, guns blazing. The Span-

On July 3, 1898, Admiral Cervera led his tiny squadron out of the safety of Santiago harbor to make a blood sacrifice for Spain's honor. Admiral Sampson's warships shot the Spanish ships to pieces.

ish ships shuddered as shell after shell struck home. Belching smoke and flame, the *Maria Teresa* staggered toward shore as Cervera tried to save his crew by beaching the ship. The *Oquendo* reeled out of line to do the same, followed soon after by the *Vizcaya.* The little destroyer *Furor* exploded; its mate, the *Plutón,* dragged toward shore in flames.

Only the fast *Cristobal Colón* steamed on, fleeing west across the blue Caribbean waters once sailed by Columbus, by the conquistadores, and by the treasure galleons of Spain's wondrous empire in the New World. Six miles (9.7 km) behind came the USS *Oregon,* powerful engines straining to make up the distance, huge guns waiting for the moment that had brought the mighty battleship across 16,000 miles (26,000 km) of ocean. For two hours they raced west beneath the midday sun; then the guns of the *Oregon* spoke. The plunging shells threw up plumes of water just astern of the *Colón.* The Spanish captain turned shoreward to beach his ship and save his crew, sons of an empire that was no more.

FOUR

AMERICAN EMPIRE

ADMIRAL CERVERA was rescued from his beached ship and brought aboard the *Iowa*. The American sailors cheered the valiant admiral whose squadron had died so bravely. With Cervera's ships destroyed, the Spanish army gave up the fight; General Toral surrendered Santiago on July 17, bringing the war in Cuba to a close.

The end came not a moment too soon for the American army, as summer rains turned the jungles into a steaming furnace and sent the fever rate skyrocketing. Clara Barton and her Red Cross workers labored with army doctors to care for thousands of sick soldiers. Meanwhile, a fresh American army landed on the south coast of Puerto Rico. Against weak Spanish opposition, it moved rapidly toward the capital, San Juan.

The war in the Caribbean was nearly over, but in the Philippines Commodore Dewey still sat on a powder keg about to explode. Since the Battle of Manila Bay on May 1,

Clara Barton (1821–1912), "the Angel of the Battlefield,"
organized nurses during the Civil War, founded
the American Red Cross in 1881, and was still smiling
in 1904 after more than forty years of tending the
victims of war and natural disaster.

German warships had ignored the American blockade, landing troops to drill on a point near the German anchorage. More than twenty thousand of General Aguinaldo's Filipino rebels surrounded Manila, anxious to fight for the capital of their new republic. Unable to force the Germans from the bay and lacking instructions to recognize Philippine independence, Dewey played for time. Finally, General Wesley Merritt's American army began arriving from California.

Manila's Spanish governor, General Firmín Jaudenes, had no desire to fight. If the Americans would agree to protect his men from Aguinaldo's rebels, he would happily surrender Manila. The Americans and the Spaniards made a deal. On the morning of August 13, Dewey's ships raised anchor and steamed toward the city. Two British warships steamed between the American battle line and the German ships on the far side of the bay, in what looked to many like a warning to the Germans to stay out of the fight. The Spaniards traded a few token shots with Dewey's ships in the name of honor, then raised a white flag. The American army moved in to take control of Manila. Aguinaldo's rebels watched in outrage as the Stars and Stripes unfurled over the city.

On the day of the "battle" of Manila no one in the Philippines knew that the United States and Spain had already agreed to end the war. While the two governments began working out the details of the peace, the American army in Cuba returned to the United States. Fever had already killed more

General Emilio Aguinaldo (1869–1964), shown here on horseback about 1900, led a bloody revolt when the United States dashed Philippine hopes for a republic. More than two hundred thousand Filipinos died in the struggle.

men than Spanish bullets. In all, some 2,000 American soldiers died of disease or accidents in the Spanish-American War; only 385 died of battlefield causes.

The Spanish-American War lasted only 113 days, but it ended one empire and began a new one. In December 1898, Spain and the United States signed a peace treaty in Paris. The United States promised to grant Cuba full independence after two years under an American military governor. Spain surrendered Puerto Rico and the Pacific island of Guam as the price of losing the war, while the United States agreed to pay a token $20 million for the Philippines.

The United States went back on its promise of complete independence for Cuba. In 1901 the Senate passed the Platt Amendment, which gave the United States veto power over most decisions of the new Cuban government. In the Philippines, the United States' refusal to recognize Aguinaldo's republic sparked a brutal war. American soldiers burned villages and crops, set up concentration camps, and shot suspected rebels without trial. The capture of Aguinaldo in March 1901 crippled the rebel leadership. When the war sputtered out a year later, 4,000 American soldiers, 20,000 rebels, and a shocking 200,000 Filipino civilians lay dead.

The experience of war cooled American enthusiasm for expansionism. The author Mark Twain, former president Grover Cleveland, industrialist Andrew Carnegie, and many other famous Americans joined the Anti-Imperialist League to argue against empire building. War had also sobered the

Under the forceful leadership of President Theodore
Roosevelt, the United States became a world power.
Here he makes very clear to a mustache-twisting diplomat
that the United States will enforce the Monroe Doctrine
barring European meddling in the Americas.

nation's new president, Theodore Roosevelt. T. R. had returned from Cuba a hero to become McKinley's vice president in 1900. Less than a year later, an assassin's bullet struck down McKinley, and Roosevelt became president. During his two terms in office, the United States built a large navy, started a canal across Panama, and increased its influence around the world. Yet Roosevelt avoided using force, preferring to "speak softly and carry a big stick."

As American power grew in the twentieth century, many smaller nations came to resent the threat of America's "big stick." Latin Americans — especially Cubans — developed a strong dislike of the United States and *Yanqui* meddling in their affairs. Filipinos spent more than forty years winning independence by peaceful means, and they guard it jealously today. Puerto Ricans have yet to decide if they want statehood, independence, or a continuation of limited self-rule as a United States commonwealth.

Americans are likewise undecided about how they want to be seen in the world. No one likes a bully; yet America's power wisely used can safeguard peace and help less fortunate nations. In this century the United States has been both generous and selfish; sometimes patient and sometimes quick to anger; often the champion of democratic values but frequently the friend of dictators. The Spanish-American war brought the United States to world power. Almost a century later, Americans are still learning how best to use that power in the making of a just and peaceful world.

SUGGESTED READING

Carroll, Raymond. *The Caribbean: Issues in U.S. Relations.* New York: Franklin Watts, 1984.

Cross, Esther, and Wilbur Cross. *Spain.* Chicago: Childrens Press, 1985.

Freidel, Frank. *The Splendid Little War.* New York: Bramhall House, 1958.

Garraty, John A. *Theodore Roosevelt: The Strenuous Life.* New York: American Heritage, 1967.

Lawson, Don. *The New Philippines.* New York: Franklin Watts, 1986.

O'Toole, G. J. A. *The Spanish War: An American Epic.* New York: Norton, 1984.

Roosevelt, Theodore. *The Autobiography of Theodore Roosevelt.* New York: Scribner's, 1958.

Vazquez, Maria B., and Rosa E. Casas. *Cuba.* Chicago: Childrens Press, 1987.

Weisberger, Bernard A. *Reaching for Empire.* New York: Time-Life, 1964.

INDEX

Page numbers in *italics* refer to illustrations.

ABOUT THE AUTHOR

ALDEN R. CARTER is a versatile writer for children and young adults. He has written nonfiction books on electronics, supercomputers, radio, Illinois, Shoshoni Indians, the American Revolution, the People's Republic of China, the Alamo, the Civil War, the Battle of Gettysburg, the Colonial Wars, the War of 1812, and the Mexican War. His novels *Growing Season* (1984), *Wart, Son of Toad* (1985), *Sheila's Dying* (1987), and *Up Country* (1989) were named to the American Library Association's annual list, Best Books for Young Adults. His fifth novel, *RoboDad,* was honored as Best Children's Fiction Book of 1990 by the Society of Midland Authors. Mr. Carter lives with his wife, Carol, and their children, Brian Patrick and Siri Morgan, in Marshfield, Wisconsin.